DINOBIBI
UNITED KINGDOM
TRAVEL FOR KIDS

Written by: Celia Jenkins

© **Copyright 2019 - Dinobibi:** All rights reserved. No part of this publication may be reproduced, stored in retrieval systems, or transmitted by any means, including electronic, mechanical, photocopying, or otherwise, without prior written permission of the publisher and copyright holder. **Disclaimer:** Although the author and Dinobibi have taken all reasonable care in preparing this book, we make no warranty about the accuracy or completeness of its content and, to the maximum extent permitted, disclaim all liability arising from its use.

CONTENTS

Native Plants & Animals (pg. 21)

Food, Culture & Traditions (pg. 25)

Famous People (pg. 35)

Major Cities & Attractions (pg. 38)

Hiya, my name's Rosie. I feel really lucky to have a normal British name, because when I was born, my Mum had a different name in mind. She wanted to call me Florence. In the UK, traditional names for girls have been popular recently, and so there are a lot of little girls called things like Agatha, Mavis, Beatrix, Edith, Iris... and a bunch of other names that would be really embarrassing! It would have been dreadful to be called Florence. Rosie is quite a common name, and sometimes my Grandpa called me Rosie Posie when he's teasing me, so I call him Grampy Stampy to get my own back, and Grandpa stamps his feet and pretends to be angry.

Grandpa is one of my favorite people in the world. I think we've been particularly close since my Grandma died, because Grandpa says that I'm a lot like her. Grandma taught me how to bake cakes, and how to do sewing, and many other things that Grandpa can't do unless I help him. Also, Grandpa likes to treat me because he knows things can be tough for me at home! I have two little brothers, Rupert and Oscar, who are twins, and they're five years old. However, they sometimes act like they're still babies and can be really naughty, so my parents are often too busy chasing after the twins to pay attention to me!

Fun Fact

London is the capital city of the UK and is known as a 'melting pot' of different cultures and ethnic groups. In the 2011 census, it was discovered that less than 50% of people living in London were 'white British.' London is one of the most ethnically diverse cities in the world.

I live in a small town called Chippenham. Don't worry, no-one has heard of it, so I won't be surprised if you don't know it either! Chippenham is in Wiltshire which is in the southwest of England, in the United Kingdom. The population is around 40,000 or 50,000 people, which sounds like a big number to me, but it's tiny compared to the cities. But my family didn't always live here. My mum's family came from Wales, and she lived there until she went to work in London, and that's where she met my dad. My dad was born in India, but his family moved to London when he was only a few months old, so although he looks Indian, he feels 100% British. When my parents got married, they moved to Chippenham because Dad had been offered a job nearby, and then my mum's parents came to live in this town, too, so we could all be together.

My dad has a job that everyone thinks is really cool, but actually it's really boring. He works for the MOD, which stands for the Ministry of Defence. When people hear that, they always ask really dumb questions like 'Is your Dad a spy?' and 'Does your Dad make bombs and tanks?' and 'Does your Dad know when World War Three will happen?' Actually, he works for the MOD but his job is just a regular IT job. He says it's an office job, just like any other boring job. Hey, I just had a thought... Maybe he is a spy, but he just can't tell me, and so he pretends he has a boring office job. I'll have to investigate!

My mum worked in retail before she got married, and she specialized in charity shops and was the manager of a big charity shop called Dorothy House. But since the twins were born, Mum has been busy trying to keep them under control and doesn't have a job any more apart from being a housewife. She often says she'd like to start doing some volunteering, but then something happens with Rupert of Oscar and she's too busy to think about it.

Like most people in the UK, my parents aren't religious. My dad's parents are Hindu, because that's the most popular religion in India, and they continued to practice it when they came to the UK. However, my dad is an atheist and so is my Mum. Her parents were raised as Christians. Grandpa came from a Catholic family, but he gave that up when he was a teenager. My grandma was part of the Church of Wales, and although she didn't go to church very often when she was older, she still said she was a Christian.

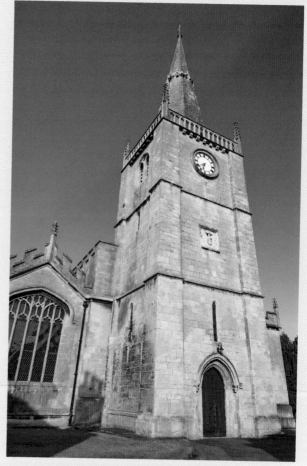

Grandpa told me he went to a strict Catholic school in Wales. I'm so glad I go to a normal, non-religious school, even if it's not a very good one. In the UK, you can pay to go to a private school which is sometimes better, but they cost a lot of money. My school in Chippenham is quite crowded, and sometimes the teachers aren't very happy with their jobs, so they quit. But for me, I like school, even if my grades aren't always so good. My grandma used to say I should have been born hundreds of years ago when girls didn't have to go to school, because I'm good at all the things housewives need to know like knitting and cleaning and cooking, but I'm not very good at learning academic subjects.

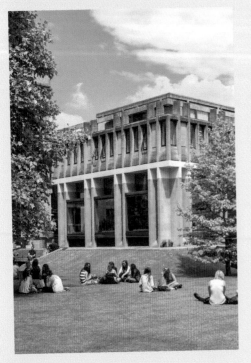

Mum got so angry when she heard Grandma say that! Mum is a housewife herself, but she always tells me that I shouldn't just think about being somebody's wife when I'm a grown up, and I should think about enjoying life for myself first. I really try my best at school, but there are some things I'm just not good at.

But I want to try my best and make my family proud, because I know my Mum hopes I'll go to university because she didn't have the chance. I don't know what I'd study at university because I don't think you can do a degree in knitting!

Perhaps I'll learn how to be a chef instead, but I don't think I need to go to university to do that. Grandpa told me that although it seems like everyone goes to university, it's not true, and less than 30% of 18-year-olds in the UK go to university. There are other places you can go to study, like community colleges. If I'm honest, I think that kind of place would be better for a practical person like me!

Before we start exploring, please tell me a few things about yourself!

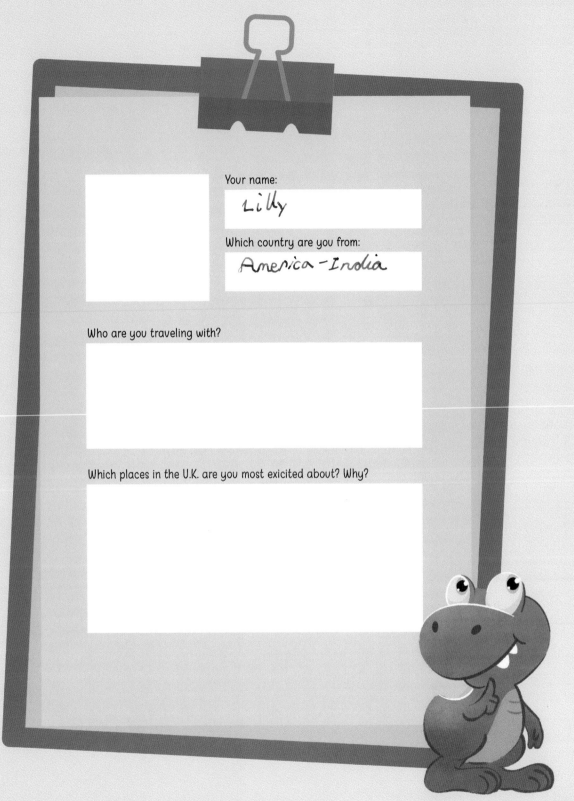

Your name:

Lilly

Which country are you from:

America - India

Who are you traveling with?

Which places in the U.K. are you most exicited about? Why?

The United Kingdom is actually several places squeezed into one. Sometimes, people think the UK and England are the same thing, and my mum gets really annoyed by that! The United Kingdom is made up of four different regions. Do you know what they are? Ok, I'll tell you. There's England, Wales, Scotland, and Northern Ireland.

The first three are all together on the same island, and then on the left there's a smaller island which is Ireland and Northern Ireland. These islands are different countries, so the UK is made up of two countries. While Ireland isn't part of the UK (just Northern Ireland), it's an important place because it's close by.

Scotland

North Sea

Atlantic Ocean

Northern Ireland

Irish Sea

England

Wales

English Channel

Do you know what the capital city of the UK is? Almost everyone knows because it's such a famous place! Our capital city is London, and it has been so since 1801. In the past, other places were called the capital, but they aren't anything like London is today, and most of them are so small that most people haven't got a clue where they are. One place in Scotland that used to be the capital is called Scone, which is really funny because we have a cake in the UK called a scone too. Nobody knows if scones come from Scone, but the first person to write about scones was a Scottish poet in the 1500's, so perhaps it's true that scones come from Scone!

Fun Fact
The biggest and most populous region of the UK is England, which has a population of around 55 million.

After London, the next biggest cities are Birmingham and Manchester, both of which are further up north. Actually, most of the cities with the biggest populations are in the North. These include West Yorkshire, the North East, Edinburgh (which is in Scotland), Liverpool, Sheffield and Glasgow (also in Scotland). The only city from Wales in the top ten is Cardiff.

Flags of the U.K.

Because the UK is split up into four different places, we have a lot of different flags too.

The Union Jack is the flag for the whole of the UK, and it is red, white, and blue. It's been the national flag since London became the capital, over 200 years ago. Then different regions have their own flags.

England's flag is red and white, and Scotland's is white and blue, but I think Wales has the best flag because it has the picture of a red dragon on it.

Th Union Jack, Flag of the UK

Flag of England   Flag of Scotland   Flag of Wales

Mountains of the U.K.

When you think about the UK, what comes to mind? You probably think about all the popular attractions in London like Big Ben, the London Eye, and Buckingham Palace. Maybe you think about very 'British' things like the Queen, cups of tea, and Beatrix Potter.

But I bet you don't really think about the landscape of the UK, because it's not as famous. Actually, the UK is a really beautiful place, and although tourists always go to the cities, there are loads of countryside places that are worth visiting.

My grandma always used to love the mountains. She couldn't do much hiking when she was old, but she liked to walk around the base of the mountain and look up and marvel at how tall it was. I think that Welsh people love the mountains because there are so many of them in Wales, and when the mist hangs over them, they look so mysterious and magical. One of the most famous mountains in Wales is Snowdon, which is over 1,000 meters tall.

When I visited it a few years ago, I remember seeing a lake that was as black as ink, and there were no ripples so you could see the clouds reflected perfectly, like a mirror. When we got to the top of the mountain, it was so misty that we couldn't see the view back down!

Llynnau Mymbyr lake located in a valley in Snowdonia

Ben Nevis

Carrauntoohil

Wales has a lot of other mountains, and their names are in Welsh so people never know how to pronounce them. My mum speaks to me in Welsh sometimes and so does my grandpa, so I can speak a bit of the Welsh language. Other nice mountains in Wales include Cadair Idris, Crib Goch, Moel Siabod, and Tryfan.

The highest mountain in the UK is Ben Nevis, which is in Scotland. It's 1,345 meters high. Actually, if you look at a list of the highest mountains in the UK, the first seventy-five are in Scotland! Number 76 is Snowdon in Wales, and then there are many, many more Scottish mountains. The first Irish mountain on the list is Carrauntoohil, which is the 133rd highest mountain in the UK, and then England doesn't make it onto the list until the mountain called Scarfell Pike, which is 978 meters tall and number 257 on the list. Wow, I really had no idea there were so many mountains in Scotland! I guess that's why Scotland is called 'the highlands.'

Rivers of the U.K.

River Thames

Perhaps you know the UK has a lot of rivers, and one of the most famous is the River Thames which goes through London. The longest river in the UK is the River Severn, which is 220 miles long. Near where I live is the River Avon, which is a really funny name because 'Avon' is an old word for river, and so it's actually called 'River River.' There's also a place in the UK called Bredon Hill, and 'Bredon' means 'Hill' in the old language, so it's called 'Hill Hill.' Language is such a funny thing!

River Severn

U.K. Currency

In the UK we use a currency called the Pound Sterling, which we just call 'pounds' for short. We have paper money and coins, and coins are just for small amounts. The pound sign is like this: £. However, in Ireland they use the Euro like many other European countries. But as Ireland is on a different island, it doesn't cause us any problems because it's not part of the UK. Northern Ireland uses the pound like we have in England. People in Scotland use the Pound like we do, but their coins and notes have different pictures on. Also, there are some small islands south of the UK called the Channel Islands, and they're also part of the UK but they have different types of coins and notes too. They even have one-pound notes, which is crazy to us in the UK because the smallest note we have is the £5 note.

In the UK, the cost of living is quite high, and although it's a developed country, a lot of people are quite poor. It really depends where you live though, because some parts of the UK are more expensive than others. London is the most expensive place to live, and other expensive places are posh cities like Bath, Oxford, Reading, and Bournemouth. Living in a small town is usually cheaper than a city, but living in a really small town or village is expensive. For example, I live in Chippenham which is a town, and so it's cheaper than the city of Bath. But nearby is a smaller town called Corsham, where my Dad works, and that place is more expensive than Chippenham. Usually, the further north you go, and the closer to Scotland you get, the cheaper it is.

Hi, it's me, Rosie. Guess what? It's raining. Again. If there's one thing that we 'Brits' love to talk about, it's the weather. Actually, we don't really talk about the weather, we moan and complain about the weather, basically all the time. British people are famously good complainers, and whenever you meet someone and don't know what to say, if you start talking about the weather then you'll soon have something in common.

If you read a tourist brochure about the UK, it might say something like 'The United Kingdom enjoys plentiful rainfall throughout the year' which makes it sound positive, but of course no one really likes the rain, do they? Does it rain a lot where you're from? Sometimes I get so fed up with the rain because it seems so endless. On average, the UK has about 130 to 150 rainy days in one year, so there are more days without rain than with rain, but it still seems like a pretty high percentage to me! If it rained for 150 days in a row, that would mean it would rain for five months!

Some places around the world have a rainy season, and then at other times it hardly rains at all. In the UK, it can rain pretty much any time, but it rains less in the summer and the autumn. Also, how much rain you get depends on where you live in the UK. It rains a lot more in the north than it does in the south, and in places like Scotland and Wales it rains a lot too. Rain, rain, rain. When I was little, my grandpa taught me a nursery rhyme that goes like this: Rain, rain, go away, come again another day.

Fun Fact

People in Britain complain about the rain, but it's certainly not the wettest place on earth. In 2011, the annual average rainfall for the UK was 1,900mm. In places like India and Hawaii, the annual average rainfall can be over 10,000 mm!

Wherever you are in the UK, the temperature is almost always cool, and the weather is usually cloudy. That's because the UK is an island (ok, it's actually two islands), so we have no protection against wind, because we're surrounded by the sea. In England, the temperature is usually around 20°C (68°F) in the summer, and 1°C (38°F) in the winter. The hottest temperature on record in the UK was 38.5°C (101°F), and the coldest ever was –27°C (–17°F), in Scotland.

Northern Ireland is a bit cooler than England. The temperature there is usually around 18.5°C (65°F) in the summer, and in the winter it's about the same. In Wales, it's similar to Northern Ireland, but Scotland is much colder. The temperature up north is usually around 17°C (65°F) in the summer, and 0°C (32°F) in the winter.

But because of global warming, things are changing. In the summer, things have been getting really hot and people can't deal with it because they're not used to it. Sometimes the weather in the UK reaches temperatures that are hotter than places like Spain! It's so funny though, because people complain whatever the weather does. If it's really cold and wet, like normal, people say 'Oh I wish it were warm and sunny.' But then if the weather is nice, people say 'Oh it's too hot, it's unnatural, I don't like it.' British people are never happy!

One thing I do like about the weather and climate in the UK is that we have four distinct seasons. My best friend in school is Gillian, and her aunt and uncle live in Thailand where they have the same weather almost all year round. Sometimes I think it would be nice to live somewhere that's always warm and sunny, and only rains in the monsoon season, but actually, I think that would get boring after a while.

In the UK, each season is different, and you can see the changes approaching that signal the start of a new one. Spring is a lovely time because all the plants start to grow and the flowers bloom, and you can see lambs in the field when it's the lambing season. You know that summer is on the way when it starts to rain less, and you can go outside without wearing a jumper (sweater). Summer means sunshine and going to the beach and eating ice-cream. Most people are sad when summer ends because it starts to get colder, but everything looks beautiful in the autumn because all the leaves on the trees go red and brown, and it's a nice time to go walking and enjoy nature. In the winter, it might be cold and dark outside but it's a nice time to spend indoors. Winter is great for drinking hot chocolate, having a nice warm bowl of soup for lunch, and sitting next to a roaring fireplace while you're reading a book.

Fun Fact

Weather in Britain is greatly affected by the 'jet stream,' which is a fast-flowing air current that makes Britain a rainy place. It flows from west to east and can make the weather change in just one day.

Are you interested in history? I know I am. The one thing that disappoints me is that there aren't more famous people in history named Rosie. Whenever I ask people if they know anyone named Rosie, they usually start singing the Rosie and Jim theme tune. Rosie and Jim was a British children's TV program on when my parents were younger, and she's the only Rosie most people know. Rosie the Riveter is also from history, but she isn't a real person. In World War 2, a lot of women in Britain took on manual jobs and worked in factories. There's a famous cartoon of a woman dressed in workman's overalls, flexing her muscles, and saying 'We Can Do It!' The cartoon is quite famous so you might have seen it. Anyway, the lady in that cartoon is called Rosie the Riveter, and it refers to women who work doing those hard jobs.

Queen Elizabeth II

The UK has a lot of famous women in its history. Right now, Queen Elizabeth II is on the throne. She is the world's longest-serving female head of state and is also the oldest and longest-reigning British monarch. In the UK, a lot of people don't like the royal family these days. People think that the royal family is a waste of money. They think it's silly and oldfashioned to have a royal family. But I think the royal family is nice. Some of them say silly things, but I think that tourists are interested in the royal family, so it's good for our country. Also, people forget that the Queen is really old. She's in her nineties, but she works hard all the time and is often going to visit people for celebrations.

Queen Elizabeth II isn't the only famous Queen in British history. Queen Victoria reigned for more than 63 years, which at the time was the longest that anybody in Britain had sat on the throne. I mean, she didn't sit on the throne for all that time, but that she was Queen for all those years! When she was Queen, the time period in Britain was known as the Victorian Era. Queen Victoria had several children, and she's famous for wearing a lot of black clothes and looking sad because she was so upset when her husband died. She never really cheered up for the rest of her life.

Fun Fact
Queen Victoria had nine children; five girls and four boys. Her children didn't like her very much!

There's another Queen you might have heard of named Queen Elizabeth (the first!) She reigned in 1558 until 1603. At that time, having a Queen on the throne wasn't normal, and everybody would have preferred to have a King. But Elizabeth's half-brother died when he was young, and because there were no more boys, she eventually got to be the Queen. She was famous because she never got married, and she said she was "married to her country."

Everyone thought that Elizabeth was a strong woman, and because her brother (and sister) had only reigned for a short time before she came to the throne, everyone was amazed that Elizabeth was the Queen for over forty years. She had bright red hair and pale white skin, and if you see portraits of her, she usually looks very glamorous and beautiful.

Queen Elizabeth's father, Henry the VIII (8th), is just as famous as she was. He is well-known because he had so many wives! That wasn't a normal thing to do in those days; once people married, they stayed married for life! But King Henry wasn't happy with his first wife because they didn't have any sons, only one daughter. It was important for the King to have a son, so he decided to get divorced so he could have a new wife would give him a son.

This caused a big, big problem in the UK because people were religious at that time and didn't believe in divorce. He asked the Pope to let him divorce Catherine, his first wife, but the pope wouldn't allow it. King Henry broke with the Catholic Church and made up his own rules so that he could get married again. In 1533, he married Anne Boleyn, but she didn't give him a son either; they had a daughter, Elizabeth, who would one day be the queen! Henry was angry with Anne and said she had committed treason and done many bad things. We will never know if the accusations were true because a King in those days could say anything he wanted, and people would believe him!

In the end, King Henry ordered Anne Boleyn to be beheaded, and he married again. This time he married a woman named Jane Seymour. Henry really loved her a lot because she gave birth to a son; the son that Henry always wanted. But then Jane died, and Henry was alone again. So… can you guess it? That's right! He got married again. In the end, King Henry the 8th got married six times. We have a rhyme to help us remember what happened to his wives. It goes like this: Divorced, beheaded, died. Divorced, beheaded, survived.

That means he divorced two of his wives, two of them had their heads chopped off, one died naturally, and the last one, Catherine Parr, survived and lived longer than he did.

Lady Jane Grey is known as the Nine Days' Queen. Henry the 8th's son, Edward, didn't want his sister Mary to be the Queen when he died, because she was a Roman Catholic.

He decided that Jane should be the Queen instead, even though she wasn't next in line. After Edward's death, Lady Jane Grey became the Queen, Mary was very angry and people took her side when she argued with the claim.

Jane was charged with high treason, and was executed at a young age.

I guess you can say I really am a royalist because instead of just talking about the history of Britain, I've been talking about the history of our royal family! There are many more interesting things to know about our history. In school, we often study about recent history, which includes World War 1 and World War 2.

But sometimes we look at ancient history too and learn about the Stone Age, the Anglo-Saxons, and the Vikings. Britain has many museums about our history. It seems you can't go anywhere without learning something new.

Pop Quiz
How long did World War 2 go on for?
a) 4 years, 3 months and 20 days
b) 6 years and 1 day
c) 7 years and 13 days

(answer (b) — 6 years and 1 day)

CHAPTER 4

NATIVE PLANTS AND ANIMALS

Roe Deer

The UK is kinda lame when it comes to flora and fauna. We don't have any big, amazing animals like lions and tigers, bears, and elephants. The wild animals that we have in the UK are usually of the small and cute variety. We don't have jungles or other exotic habitats on this little island, either. Most of the wildlife we have likes to live in forests or mountains, but some of the animals live near cities now.

One of the biggest animals we have is the deer. While there are six types of deer living in the UK,

only two of those types are native: The Roe deer and the Scottish red deer. The Roe deer can be a red colour, or more like a brown or grey, and they aren't very big. You get this kind of deer all over Europe, so they aren't particularly special. The Scottish red deer are even smaller. Although you see a lot of these deer in Scotland, you can find them all over the UK and even near where I live, in Wiltshire. They have big antlers and, in the winter, they grow long fur on their neck to keep warm.

Fun Fact

The other types of deer found in the UK are called Fallow, Water, Sika and Reeve's Muntjac.

There are several woodland parks in the U.K. where tourist and photographers can get to see deers in their natural environment.

If you live near the coast, you might get to see a grey seal. The Latin version of their name means 'hooked-nose pig' which I think fits really well because they do look a bit like ocean pigs! Although the whole of the UK is a popular place for the grey seal to live, they also swim to other places in Northern Europe where the water is even colder. The baby seal is called a pup, and it is really cute. However, the adult seals are noisy and are only graceful in the water; on land, they look like they're stuck!

Grey Seal

British Hedgehog

In recent years, people in the UK have taken more of an interest in wildlife because of TV programs such as Country File and Spring Watch . These shows encourage people to look in their own gardens and see what they can find. People are happier to see some animals than others. For example, most people like to find a hedgehog in their garden because they're small and cute. Hedgehogs are covered in spikes called spines. When they're frightened, hedgehogs, roll into a ball with all the spines on the outside to protect them.

My brothers, Rupert and Oscar, don't like cute animals. They like animals that look scary, like snakes. We don't have many snakes in the UK. In fact, in Britain we only have the adder. The adder is a venomous snake, but it's not aggressive. Once Rupert found an adder in the garden and tried to frighten me by saying it would bite me. But I wasn't frightened at all because I knew the adder wouldn't hurt me.

Other animals that you can often see are squirrels, rabbits, and otters. Less common are nocturnal (night time) animals like badgers and foxes. In fact, you often see foxes in cities because they like to find food that humans have left out. Urban foxes will climb into people's dustbins and rip open the rubbish bags to find food. People throw away so much food that doing this might be easier for a fox than trying to hunt in the wild.

Fun Fact
It's estimated that around 33,000 foxes live in London!

Native Plant Life

Goat Willow Tree in Bloom

Britain has a mild climate with a warm summer and a cold winter which means we can grow different types of plants and not just native types of plant. If you have a greenhouse, you can grow exotic plants too. A many different types of willow trees are native to the UK, such as goat willow, almond willow, bay willow and grey willow. I like dogwood because the flower (which has four white petals) is so pretty and delicate. My grandpa likes gorse, which is bright yellow and grows near the ocean. Yellow is his favorite colour, and he often wears his favorite yellow sweater, although Mum says it's really called mustard colour.

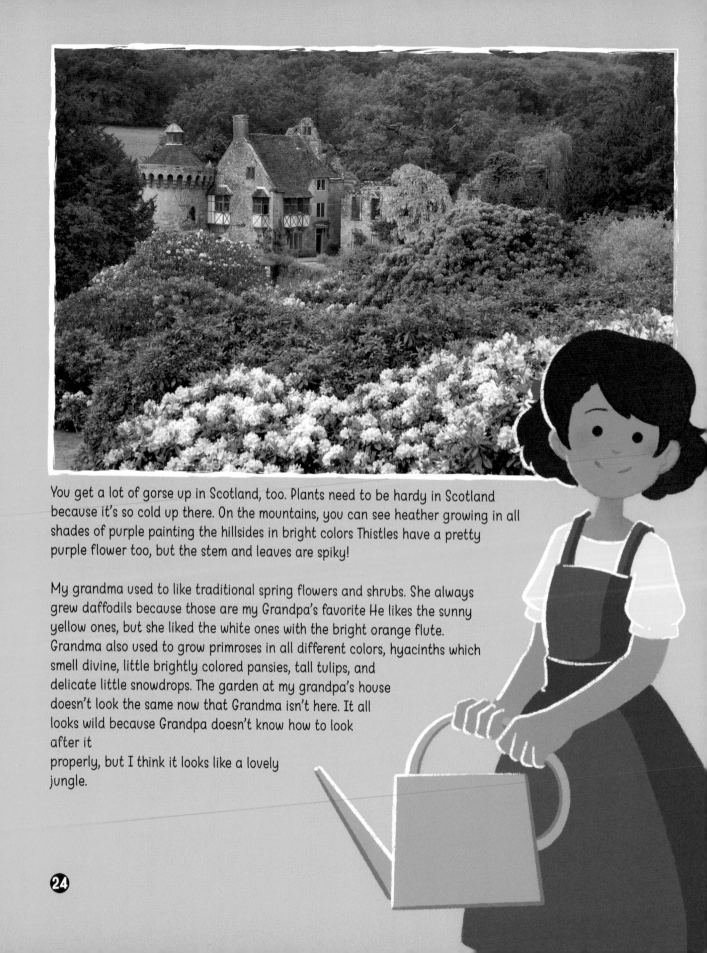

You get a lot of gorse up in Scotland, too. Plants need to be hardy in Scotland because it's so cold up there. On the mountains, you can see heather growing in all shades of purple painting the hillsides in bright colors Thistles have a pretty purple flower too, but the stem and leaves are spiky!

My grandma used to like traditional spring flowers and shrubs. She always grew daffodils because those are my Grandpa's favorite He likes the sunny yellow ones, but she liked the white ones with the bright orange flute. Grandma also used to grow primroses in all different colors, hyacinths which smell divine, little brightly colored pansies, tall tulips, and delicate little snowdrops. The garden at my grandpa's house doesn't look the same now that Grandma isn't here. It all looks wild because Grandpa doesn't know how to look after it properly, but I think it looks like a lovely jungle.

CHAPTER 5

FOOD, CULTURE, AND TRADITIONS

What do you think of when you think of Britain? For most people, one thing that springs to mind is a nice cup of tea! The British have been drinking tea since the 1600's, but we don't all drink it the same way. Some people have their tea with milk whereas others have it with a slice of lemon. Iced tea isn't very popular in Britain, even in the summer people would usually rather a hot cup of tea than a cold one. Some people have their tea with sugar, too.

A strong cup of tea with milk is called 'builders tea.' Because everyone has their tea differently, it can be tricky to know how to make perfect cup. My grandpa likes it weak with a lot of milk while my parents like strong tea with hardly any milk in it.

In the UK, some people have many cups of tea in one day. I don't think it's good to drink cup after cup of tea because it has caffeine in and will keep you awake at night. In my opinion, three or four cups in one day is more than enough! My mum likes a cup of coffee in the morning, but she drinks tea in the afternoon. Sometimes we have tea with a biscuit or a slice of cake. A 'Cream Tea' is when you have a very fancy cup of tea with a scone, which will come with jam and cream. 'High Tea' is similar but with even more types of cakes to choose from. There's also 'Afternoon Tea' which I think means the same thing. Recently I went to my friend's house, and my parents came with me. We were all having tea and cakes and my friend's dad poured the tea. When he picked up the teapot, he said "Shall I be Mother?" I didn't know what that meant at the time. Mum told me that it's a joke people make when they're pouring tea, because usually it's the mother who serves the drinks.

In cultures around the world, people have traditional dances and music they perform at special events. People don't do much dancing in the UK now, unless they like to go to a club or a bar in the evening. Grandpa says the dancing they do in a club isn't proper dancing so that doesn't count. But different places in the UK sometimes practice their traditional dances; they're just not very popular with young people.

One traditional dance is Morris Dancing. The dancers have colorful handkerchiefs or sticks that they wave around. It's a folk dance but I think it looks more like stepping than dancing. The Morris Dancers don't look very energetic or graceful.

Irish Dancing — A traditional dance that is totally different is Irish Dancing, which comes from Ireland. The dancers stand very straight and have their arms flat down by their sides. When they dance, they kick their legs up high into the air. Irish Dancers wear tap shoes so their feet make a click-clack sound on the ground. When the famous show, Riverdance, came out, it introduced a lot of people to Irish dancing.

British people are famous for queuing. Have you heard that? When I found out that this is something we're famous for I was very surprised that it was unique. I mean, if you don't queue nicely, then everybody will just push to get to the front. In the past, British people were well-known for being polite. Perhaps queuing up and waiting your turn is our way of being polite.

We have many traditions that relate to food in the UK. It's a popular custom to go to the pub, which is the short name for a 'public house.' This place is where you go in the evening to buy a drink, but on the weekend many people go in the daytime, too. It's popular to go for a long walk in the countryside and then go and have lunch at a pub.

Sunday lunch is one of the busiest times at a pub. Many pubs serve a carvery on Sunday, or what we call a roast dinner.

A lot of British families will have 'a roast' every week for Sunday lunch. A roast dinner includes roast meat (usually beef, pork, lamb or chicken, or turkey at Christmas), roast potatoes, roast vegetables (like carrots and parsnips), Yorkshire puddings (which are little pancakes shaped like a cup), gravy (which is a dark, meaty sauce), other vegetables (like boiled peas or Brussel sprouts) and then another type of sauce depending on which meat you have (horseradish with beef, cranberry with turkey, mint with lamb, applesauce with pork, and anything you like with chicken).

My grandpa is traditional and likes to have a roast every Sunday. My grandma used to make lovely roast dinners but Grandpa can't do it by himself. It would be too much food just for one person. Sometimes Grandpa comes to see us on a Sunday, so we make a special roast dinner for him, even though we don't usually make them. On the other weeks, he meets his friends and has lunch at the pub!

Birthdays and Fairy Cakes

Don't you just love birthday parties? My friend Gillian's party is this weekend, and I can't wait. Today Mum and I went shopping and bought her a present. I wanted to get her some chocolate, but Mum said that it would be better to get something fun and practical.

We went to the hobby shop and bought a craft kit. Mum helped me wrap it in a piece of sparkly pink wrapping paper but she said that this is the last time we will buy sparkly paper because it can't be recycled like normal wrapping paper. We're trying to be more eco-friendly, even on birthdays!

Gillian always has amazing birthday parties. Her parents have a house with a big garden, and they always hire a bouncy house. Last year, her bouncy castle was a big pink princess castle. She had a birthday cake that looked like a unicorn, and it had edible sparkles on it!

The cake is the most important part about birthdays in the UK. Recently, people have been making all sorts of amazing cakes. Sometimes people don't have one big cake and instead they have a tower of cupcakes. Actually, cupcake is an American word; in the UK we call them fairy cakes.

Christmas Traditions –
In the UK, Christmas is the most important holiday, even though it's a Christian festival and not everybody is Christian. I know that most people always want to see snow on Christmas Day, but that rarely happens here.

Fun Fact
It doesn't often snow in December in the UK; it's far more likely to snow in January or February.

What are your Christmas traditions? For me, the best part of the day is Christmas lunch. Some people eat their Christmas meal in the evening, but my dad says it's better to eat it at lunchtime because then you have time to digest it! We usually get a turkey; it's the only time of year we get one! I don't like turkey very much because it gets dry easily. However, the traditional feeling of seeing a turkey on the dinner table can't be beaten!

Grandma and Grandpa used to stay at home and cook their own meal because Grandma didn't like turkey. However, since Grandma passed away, Grandpa has been coming to see us on Christmas Day. He likes the turkey, but there is one part of the meal he hates. I was so surprised when he told me because it's one of my favorite bits of the meal... the bread sauce! We don't eat it at any other time of year. It's a thick, gloopy sauce made out of bread. The taste is creamy and mild, and it goes well with the turkey!

One of my favorite things to eat at Christmas is gingerbread. I used to make it with my grandma, and we would give it to people as presents. You can make gingerbread men all year round, although now we call them 'gingerbread people' to be more politically correct! However, it's only at Christmas that you make a gingerbread house. It's really tricky! A gingerbread house has to be glued together in pieces using icing. Then you decorate it with sweeties and chocolate. You want to put as many sweeties as possible on the roof, but if you put too many it will break.

Fun Fact
Although gingerbread houses are popular in the UK, gingerbread actually originated from Germany!

We have many smaller festivals in the UK, too. Guy Fawkes is a great event, and it's nice to have something fun to look forward to in the autumn. Guy Fawkes was a man living in the 1600's. He plotted to kill the King, but his plan failed. In memory of this, we make big dolls that look like Guy Fawkes and burn them on big bonfires. We also set off fireworks and eat snacks like candy apples. Sometimes people make Guy Fawkes dolls that look like other people, even celebrities. I like going to look at all the different dolls before they're set on fire.

Before the start of Lent, we have a festival called Pancake Day. During Lent, people are supposed to give up things they like for forty days. Before Lent starts, you should use up all the eggs and sugar in your house, and that's why people make pancakes. The holiday is also called Shrove Tuesday because it always falls on the second day of the week. When people make the pancakes they sometimes flip them up into the air. I've heard about pancake filling contest, but I don't think I'd be very good at it! Grandpa tried to help me with flipping a pancake last year, and we dropped it on the floor!

In Scotland, one of the most interesting festivals is Up Helly Aa. The festival, which is inspired by the island's viking history, takes place on the last Tuesday in January and is the biggest fire festival in Europe!

Every year, a viking ship replica is built for the festival. Come nightfall, participants goes into a torch light procession and sing the traditional Up Helly Aa song around the ship replica. They will then throw their torches at the ship and party all night long!

In Wales, there is a festival called Eisteddfod. It's a competition of music and poetry, but we don't celebrate it in England. When I was little, Grandma and Grandpa sometimes asked me to read poetry to them. We called it a Mini Eisteddfod!

Fish and Chips – It's Friday night… that means fish and chips! In the UK a lot of families like the tradition of getting fish and chips on a Friday night because of an old Christian tradition where people wouldn't eat meat on a Friday, so they'd eat fish instead. Many families have let it become a habit that they will go to the chip shop on a Friday evening. If we were clever we would pick a different night for fish and chips. The chip shop is always busy on a Friday evening! Cod is the most popular fish, but I like to get fishcakes or scampi. My Dad doesn't always get fish either, sometimes he gets a battered sausage. My Mum always gets fish, though. Do you know what we call the fish and chip shop? We call it 'the chippy'!

Fish n' Chips

I guess it sounds quite boring to eat the same thing every week, but we actually have (omit) a varied diet. Because my dad's family came from India, he grew up eating a lot of curry. We eat curry at least once a week, but my little brothers don't like it much. Dad likes spicy curry like vindaloo, but Mum prefers a creamy curry like korma. My favorite is a tikka curry which actually doesn't come from India — it was invented in England so people in the UK could try Indian food even if they didn't like something too spicy. People usually eat curry with rice or naan bread. If I can, I like to have both! Plain naan bread is popular, but you can get naan bread that's stuffed with other ingredients. Garlic naan is delicious, and so is peshwari naan, which is stuffed with sweet spices with coconut and sultanas.

My mum used to eat a bland diet when she lived at home, but she really learned to love cooking when she moved to London. Many people in London are from different places all over the world, and they all have different cuisines. In London, you can get pretty much anything you want to eat if you travel to the right area! Mum said that when she lived in London, she would eat a different cuisine every night of the week. She didn't go to restaurants often, but she made friends with people from all over the world, and they enjoyed cooking together. Then she met my Dad, and they cooked curry together all the time

Different places across the UK have different traditional meals. In Wales, their traditional dish is so boring. I mean, it's tasty, but it's nothing special. It's called Welsh rarebit which sounds like Welsh rabbit, but it's got nothing to do with bunny rabbits. The dish is cheese sauce melted on toast. That's it! I always laugh when I think about fine dining, like French cuisine, which can take hours to prepare. To make Welsh rarebit only takes five minutes!

Fun Fact
Other names of Welsh Rarebit are Welsh Rabbit, Buck Rabbit, and Golden Buck. Some variants are called Scotch Rabbit, English Rabbit, Le Welsh, and even Blushing Bunny!

In Scotland one of the most well-known dishes is haggis. It's a savory meat pudding that's made out of the liver, heart, and lungs of a sheep, mixed with onion and other vegetables. It sounds disgusting, right? But many people like it even though it has a strong flavor I've never tried it but I'm quite adventurous so I think I would give it a go!

My favorite sausage dish is 'toad in the hole'. This is when you cook the sausages in a dish and surround them with pancake batter. As it cooks, the pancake batter rises up and covers the sausages, so they're just peeping out of the top of the mixture. I guess it's called toad in the hole because the sausage looks like a little frog in his house!

In Ireland, one of the most famous dishes is stew. A stew is like a soup, but it's much thicker and you often eat it with bread. Potatoes have been grown in Ireland for a long time. They are one of the main ingredients that go into Irish stew, along with other root vegetables and some meat.

In general, dishes in England are quiet hearty and heavy. We like potatoes in England too, and my brother Rupert's favorite meal is 'bangers and mash.' This means sausages and potatoes and it's often served with a dark gravy.

I think that the UK can be a bit boring when it comes to lunch and dinner. However, breakfast is better in the UK than anywhere else in the world! In Europe, people have a continental breakfast. That usually means cold things like cereal, cheese, bread, and pastries. And then if you look at places abroad, like China and Japan, many people eat rice for breakfast! In the UK, most people usually have a small breakfast like toast or cereal. But on the weekends, a lot of people like to have a traditional English breakfast, which is big and served hot. Many 'Full English' breakfast meals are so big that you don't need any lunch afterwards! The meal includes: sausages, bacon, toast or fried bread, eggs (scrambled, poached or fried), tomato, fried mushrooms, a hash brown (which is a potato cake), baked beans, black pudding... it's a feast!

Do you follow any celebrities? Not me. A lot of my classmates like to read about their favorite singers or actors almost every day. They follow them on Twitter and Instagram, too. I like watching films, but I'm not bothered about who stars in them. Anyway, I think that being famous for singing or acting isn't very special. I'd rather read about people who are famous for doing something amazing.

At school we've been learning about the suffragette movement in the UK because it was recently the 100 th anniversary of women getting the vote. Well, not all women; I learned that in the beginning only some women were allowed to vote, so it was still unfair. Isn't it crazy that there are still places in the world where women can't vote? Women in Saudi Arabia were only given the vote in 2015, and there are places where women are allowed to vote, but they have to ask permission from their dad or husband.

One place that women still can't vote is the Vatican City in Rome. To me that's the craziest thing because Christians are supposed to think that we're all equal. If God loves women the same as men, why can't women vote too? It's mad!

Anyway, I'm interested in the women from history who started the suffragette movement. These were people who thought that votes should be equal for men and women. At the time, many people disagreed with them, but they fought until they won the vote.

Emmeline Pankhurst is one of the most famous suffragettes, and her daughters supported her too. What's interesting is that her husband agreed with her, even though many men at the time didn't want women to have the vote.

Another suffragette you might have heard of is Emily Davidson. The suffragettes wanted the King to take notice of their campaign, but he wouldn't listen. So Emily Davidson went to a horse race and stepped in front of the King's horse during a race. The horse knocked her down, and she was killed, which made a lot of people pay attention to the fight for votes for women.

To have been a suffragette in the early 1900's must have been a difficult thing; those women were certainly brave and strong. I'm always interested in learning about women who broke the rules. Why do what everyone else does? In the late 1800's, there was a traveller and writer who broke all the rules. Her name was Gertrude Bell. At that time, people expected women to get married, have children, and not go on adventures. But Gertrude was different. She started by going to university which wasn't something women were normally permitted to do. They could only study certain subjects, and Gertrude chose history. She was the first female student to pass her degree with first class honors, so she must have been really smart.

After university Gertrude went abroad. She visited her uncle in Persia and fell in love with the country. This started many years of traveling and language learning; Gertrude was fluent in five languages and could speak a bit of two more! Incredible! She wrote books and took pictures of her travels. Later she got involved in politics and worked on important projects during the war. Not many people know about Gertrude Bell, but I think she's really fascinating.

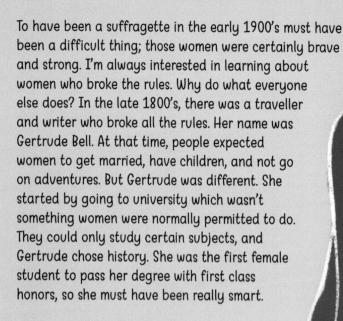

Fun Fact
During the time she served in the military, Gertrude Bell was the only woman working for the British government in the Middle East. A movie titled "Queen of the Desert" was even made based on her life.

Because I have Indian heritage, I like to find out about Indian celebrities. There aren't many historical figures from India in the UK because the two countries are a long way apart! However, I discovered that a very famous British person once made friends with an Indian person. The celebrity was Queen Victoria; I've told you about her before. Queen Victoria was called the Empress of India, and she had control over the country, even though it was far away. Her Indian friend was a servant called Mohammed Abdul Karim. The Queen noticed how smart he looked and how polite he was. She asked him to teach her the Urdu language, and she wanted to learn all about his culture.

But not everyone was so happy about this friendship. Queen Victoria was a widower and had been very sad since her husband died. People in the royal family weren't happy that she had a close relationship with an Indian man. But she found him intelligent, and they shared intellectual conversations, both in person and by letter. She called him 'the Munshi' and always wanted him by her side, even though it made her family jealous.

"The Royal Servant" is a painting of The Munshi commissioned by Her Majesty, Queen Victoria in 1887.

Fun Fact

After meeting Karim, Queen Victoria wanted to try an Indian curry!

Sadly, the story doesn't end well. Karim served the queen for fourteen years. When she died, Queen Victoria's family sent Karim and his family back to India. They destroyed the letters he had received from the Queen, and Karim was heartbroken to be treated so badly. However, there was some good news; in 2010 a secret diary of Karim's describing his time working for the Queen was discovered.

Throughout history, some of the most interesting people are those who have faced hardships because of who they are. Emmeline Pankhurst and Emily Davidson were treated badly because they were women. The Munshi was treated badly because he was from India. Queen Victoria's servant John Brown was treated badly because he wasn't from the upper classes. Whether it's gender, race, or wealth, people always find ways to discriminate and mark people out as different.

I didn't think about these things when I was little. Now that I'm older I try to think about it more. It's important to me because I'm mixed race, which makes me different to other people. My dad is from India and has dark skin, whereas my mum is Welsh and has very pale skin. I'm somewhere in the middle! Also, I know that because I'm a girl I'll have a different experience in life to my brothers. So I like looking for role models who broke the rules and fought for what they believed in. I hope they can inspire me to be brave and strong like them!

Visitors to the UK always go straight to London. I don't get it! Ok, so London has some cool attractions such as Big Ben, Buckingham Palace, the London Eye, etc. But it's always so busy and crowded in London. How can you enjoy anything when there are so many people around? Also, London is expensive. One night at a hotel in London is the same as a whole weekend in other places around the UK.

Fun Fact
Tollymore forest has been used as a filming location for the popular tv series "Game of Thrones".

I've never been to Ireland, but I really want to go. My mum and dad went to Ireland for a holiday when they were first married, and they said it was incredible. There's a place called Tollymore Forest Park which is so beautiful. There are thick forests of trees, impressive mountains and glittering lakes; it sounds perfect.

Somewhere else I'd like to visit in Ireland is the Giant's Causeway. The name comes from a legend where an Irish giant wanted to fight a Scottish giant. They built the causeway between the two places so the giants could have their fight. The rock formation looks amazing, like a beehive or hundreds of puzzle pieces on top of each other.

Have you ever heard of the Lake District? Well, if you like spending time around water then it's the number one place you should go to in the UK. The Lake District is up north, near to Scotland. It became really popular after Beatrix Potter became a famous author. She used some of her money to buy land in the Lake District and save it from being developed. While she's famous for writing books like Peter Rabbit , Beatrix Potter was also really interested in the environment. A lot of people think it's thanks to her we still have the Lake Districts.

Scotland is another place I'd like to go to. With amazing natural beauty, it would be great fun to go hiking in the mountains and see an incredible view from the top. I don't like cities much, but I'd like to go to Edinburgh because of the castle. It's one of the oldest fortified palaces in Europe and even today the military uses parts of the castle. Another reason to go to Edinburgh is for the Edinburgh Tattoo. This is a military event where people are marching and playing instruments. I've seen it on TV, and the sound is unbelievable, especially when they play the bagpipes!

The longest lake is Lake Windermere; it's more than 10 miles long! Derwentwater Lake is the third biggest, and it's very pretty. You can walk around the lake in about four hours. Some of the lakes have really funny names: Brotherswater, Crummock Water, Thirlmere, Bassenthwaite Lake, and Haweswater are my favorites In the Lake District, they also have a special word for a small lake or a pool, which is 'tarn'.

Fun Fact
The Lake District National Park was established in 1951, and extended in 2016.

One tourist locale that isn't far from where I live is the city of Bath, only a 20 min train ride from my house. Sometimes Mum and I have a 'girls' day' where just the two of us go to Bath for shopping, because there are many more shops than we have in our town. We try to go early in the morning because as the day goes on the city gets busier and busier. Bath is an interesting place because the whole city is a UNESCO World Heritage Site. Usually, it's just one thing that gets UNESCO classification. But for Bath, the whole place has the status because of the architecture and history. Bath is a Roman city. The Romans built Roman Baths supplied with naturally hot water from thermal springs. Today you can visit the Baths or even go to the modern spa to try out the water!

Bath is a city in a pudding bowl, that's what my Grandpa says! What he means is that the city is built into a dip and is surrounded by steep hills. Because of this, the centre of the city can't expand because there's nowhere for it to go. The whole city has been built in Georgian sandstone which sparkles like gold in the sunshine.

Mum and I once went to the fashion museum, even though the entry ticket was really expensive. I saw a black dress that had been worn by Queen Victoria! Another museum I like is the Holburne Museum which has a lot of nice pieces of artwork. My mum's favorite is the Victoria Art Gallery which is named after... yes, you've guessed it! Queen Victoria.

Do you know what the capital of Wales is? It's Cardiff! We go to Cardiff at least once a year because it's near where my mum grew up. Grandpa likes to visit there too. Cardiff is quite a big city, but it doesn't feel too crowded. It's a nice place to visit because it has a mixture of old and new things to see. Cardiff Castle is one of the most beautiful castles I've ever been to. There's a special tour you can go on into these amazingly furnished rooms. When we went, it was just Dad and me on the tour — Rupert and Oscar were too small, so they weren't allowed to go.

Fun Fact

In Cardiff there is an old church called the Norwegian Church Arts Centre, which was where the author Roald Dahl was baptized. He wrote book you have probably read like Charlie and the Chocolate Factory and James and the Giant Peach.

When we have a family day out, we usually go somewhere small and local. We're members of the National Trust, which is a charity that looks after old properties and natural places. There's a village near where I lived called Lacock. The Lacock Abbey is an amazing building, and it has some pretty gardens, too. Because the town and the abbey are so picturesque, Lacock is often used as a film set for popular movies. Some parts of Harry Potter were filmed in Lacock, and so were things set in the past like Pride and Prejudice and Downton Abbey . I like visiting Lacock with Grandpa because he always treats me to an ice-cream or a cream tea. The last time we went to Lacock, Grandpa tried a special local cake called a lumb. It was like a cross between a muffin and a crumpet, and there were three of them all stacked on top of each other! I told Grandpa that he wouldn't be able to finish it all himself, but he proved me wrong and gobbled the whole thing up!

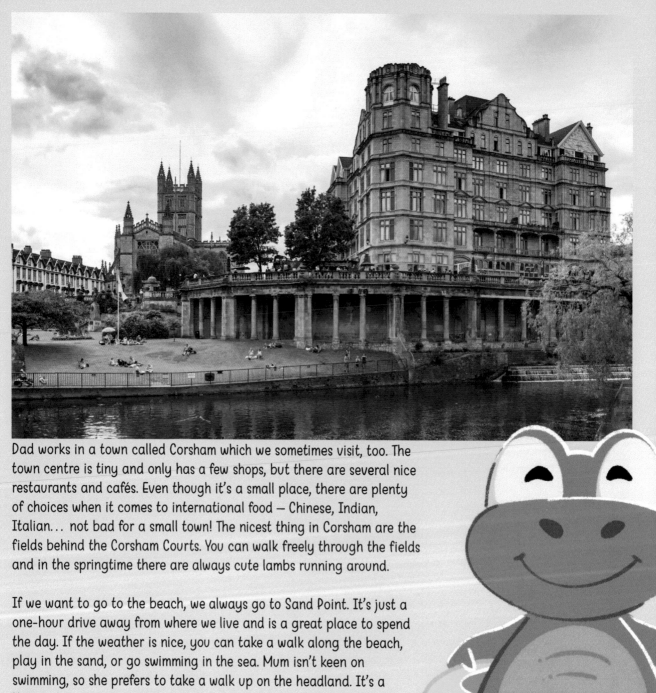

Dad works in a town called Corsham which we sometimes visit, too. The town centre is tiny and only has a few shops, but there are several nice restaurants and cafés. Even though it's a small place, there are plenty of choices when it comes to international food — Chinese, Indian, Italian... not bad for a small town! The nicest thing in Corsham are the fields behind the Corsham Courts. You can walk freely through the fields and in the springtime there are always cute lambs running around.

If we want to go to the beach, we always go to Sand Point. It's just a one-hour drive away from where we live and is a great place to spend the day. If the weather is nice, you can take a walk along the beach, play in the sand, or go swimming in the sea. Mum isn't keen on swimming, so she prefers to take a walk up on the headland. It's a National Trust area, and the coastal paths are well maintained. We once went further down the coast to Weston-super-Mare. Honestly? It was dreadful! Everyone thinks it will be fun to go there because of the pier, the beach, and the funfair. Rupert and Oscar liked it, but I thought there were too many people, and it was far too noisy! Also, the beach isn't good quality. The sand isn't nice and golden like on a good beach. In fact, the sand is so brown and yucky that everyone calls it eston-super-Mud!

CONCLUSION

People always get this idea in their heads of what the United Kingdom is like, as if it can be rolled into one neat little package. People think of the Queen and her corgis, tea with milk and sugar, greasy packets of fish and chips, the London Eye, and David Beckham. But people don't always think about the things that really matter to us 'Brits,' such as the different languages we speak, as well as regional dialects and accents. People don't think of Irish stew, Welsh Rarebit, haggis, or steak and kidney pie.

When you think of British people, do you imagine pale-skinned, light-haired people like the royal family? People often forget that British people come in all shapes, sizes, and colors — people with black hair, brown, grey, blonde, red and many other colors besides. People with white skin and dark skin, and those who are in between, like me! We don't all think the same, either. Some of us like the royal family, and some don't. Some agree with the political leaders, and others aren't so sure. While we don't agree on everything, I think British people can still find things to be united about, whether they are English, Scottish, Welsh, Irish or something else entirely.

Whatever you think about the UK and its inhabitants I hope you enjoy your visit here. Let us surprise you with things you didn't know you'd find. Be open to new experiences and, like my inspiring role models, be strong and brave! Wherever I go in life, that's my motto!

Which parts of the United Kingdom did you like the most and why?	What activities did you enjoy most and why?

Now, to the UK quiz! Good luck!

Welsh is one of the official languages of Wales, but how many people in the UK can speak it?

a) 400,000
b) 700,000
c) 1,000,000

(answer (b) – 700,000)

In cold weather, where in the UK is most likely to get snow?

a) Scotland
b) England
c) Northern Ireland

(answer (a) – Scotland)

Because the UK gets a lot of rain, floods are quite common. But which of these cities is the most likely to experience flooding?

a) Bath
b) Hull
c) Cardiff

(answer (b) – Hull)

Which type of squirrel has a population of 2.5 million in the UK?

a) Grey squirrel
b) Red squirrel
c) Pink squirrel

(answer (a) – Grey Squirrel)

In the 1950's to the 1970's, which animal almost disappeared in Britain?

a) Hedgehogs
b) Deer
c) Otters

(answer (c) – Otters)

In British culture, what is a 'tea break'?

a) When you drop your tea pot and it smashes
b) A tv commercial
c) When you take a break and have a cup of tea

(answer (c) – When you take a break and have a cup of tea.)

Which roast meat is it traditional to eat on Christmas day?

a) Turkey
b) Chicken
c) Duck

(answer (a) – Turkey)

What's the name of a British pie that has lamb in it?

a) Shepherd's Pie
b) Cottage Pie
c) Fish Pie

(answer (a) – Shepherd's Pie)

Which UK attraction is the most popular, with over 6 million visitors every year?

a) Stonehenge
b) Edinburgh Castle
c) The British Museum

(answer (c) – The British Museum)

Which British celebrity author wrote the Harry Potter series?

a) JK Rowling
b) Zadie Smith
c) Jacqueline Wilson

(answer (a) – JK Rowling)

I have thoroughly enjoyed this journey through France with you.
Feel free to visit us at www.dinobibi.com and check out our other titles!

Dinobibi Travel for Kids

Dinobibi History for Kids

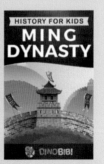

Printed in Great Britain
by Amazon

36460794R00026